NEYMAR

BY BRIAN TRUSDELL

SportsZone

An Imprint of Abdo Publishing
abdopublishing.com

abdopublishing.com

Published by Abdo Publishing, a division of ABDO, PO Box 398166, Minneapolis, Minnesota 55439. Copyright © 2018 by Abdo Consulting Group, Inc. International copyrights reserved in all countries. No part of this book may be reproduced in any form without written permission from the publisher. SportsZone™ is a trademark and logo of Abdo Publishing.

Printed in the United States of America, North Mankato, Minnesota
042017
092017

THIS BOOK CONTAINS RECYCLED MATERIALS

Cover Photo: Andreas Gebert/picture-alliance/dpa/AP Images
Interior Photos: Andreas Gebert/picture-alliance/dpa/AP Images, 1; Soeren Stache/picture-alliance/dap/AP Images, 4–5; Kyodo/AP Images, 6; Jorge Araujo/AP Images, 9; Andre Penner/AP Images, 10–11, 22–23; Cesar Olmedo/AP Images, 12; Nelson Antoine/Fotoarena/Agencia Estado/AP Images, 14; Javier Calvelo/AP Images, 16–17; Manu Fernandez/AP Images, 19; Emilio Morenatti/AP Images, 21; Niviere/Chamussy/Sipa/AP Images, 25; Bernat Armangue/AP Images, 26; Alvaro Barrientos/AP Images, 28

Editor: Todd Kortemeier
Series Designer: Craig Hinton

Publisher's Cataloging-in-Publication Data

Names: Trusdell, Brian, author.
Title: Neymar : soccer superstar / by Brian Trusdell.
Other titles: Soccer superstar
Description: Minneapolis, MN : Abdo Publishing, 2018. | Series: Playmakers |
    Includes bibliographical references and index.
Identifiers: LCCN 2017930231 | ISBN 9781532111501 (lib. bdg.) |
    ISBN 9781680789355 (ebook)
Subjects: LCSH: Neymar, 1992- --Juvenile literature. | Soccer players
    --Brazil--Biography--Juvenile literature.
Classification: DDC 796.334 [B]--dc23
LC record available at http://lccn.loc.gov/2017930231

TABLE OF CONTENTS

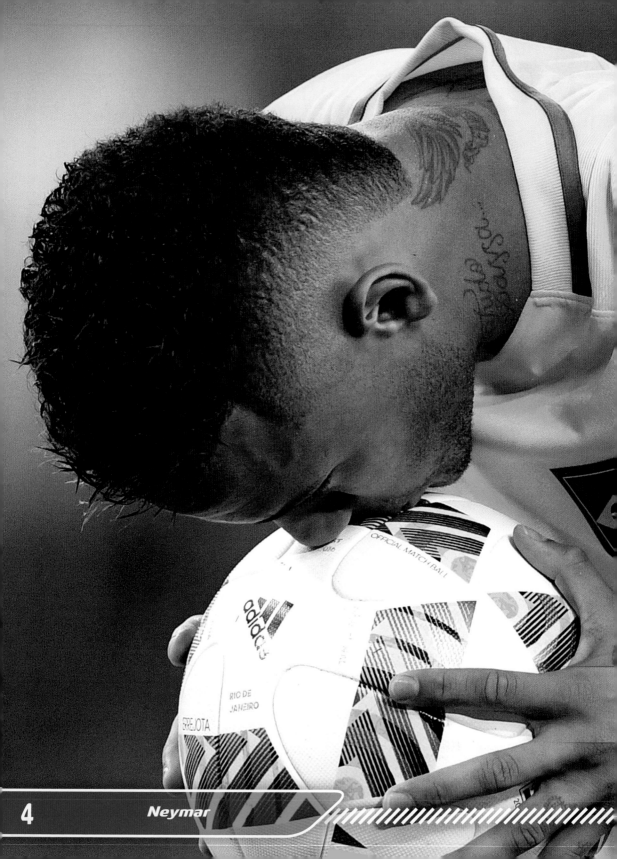

Neymar

CHAPTER 1

SPOTTED AT AN EARLY AGE

Neymar limped slightly. He had injured his leg earlier in the game. It still bothered him. His Brazil national team was facing Germany. It was the final of the 2016 Olympics. And it was at the Maracanã Stadium in Rio de Janeiro. This was the home of soccer in Brazil.

The match had gone to a penalty shootout. And now it was Neymar's turn. He put the ball on the penalty spot. Brazilian goalkeeper Weverton had just

Neymar kisses the ball just before taking the decisive penalty kick at the 2016 Summer Olympics final.

Neymar, *left*, celebrates with Brazil teammate Weverton after his gold medal-winning penalty kick.

blocked an attempt by Nils Petersen of Germany. It was up to Neymar. If he scored, Brazil would win the Olympic gold medal.

Neymar took a few steps back. He stood inside the penalty arc. He took a few steps to his left. The referee blew his whistle. Neymar ran up to the ball. He paused before picking up speed. German goalkeeper Timo Horn had to make a move. He dived low to his right to block the shot. But Neymar had shot the other way. The ball rocketed high into the left corner of the net.

Neymar dropped to his knees. He pointed to the sky with both hands. Teammates ran up and surrounded him. They were Olympic gold medalists.

Neymar da Silva Santos Jr. was born on February 5, 1992. His father was a pro soccer player in the Brazilian city of Mogi das Cruzes. It is a city of approximately 400,000 people. It is about 25 miles (40 km) from Brazil's largest city of São Paulo.

Neymar Sr. wasn't a star. His playing career lasted only a few years. When he retired, he took his family back to his hometown of São Vicente. They moved in with Neymar Sr.'s parents. Neymar Sr. worked three jobs. He was an auto mechanic, a bricklayer, and he worked for the city. His wife worked as a cook. She also took care of their children.

Neymar Jr. played soccer whenever he could. Sometimes that meant playing in the streets. He and his friends didn't always have a real ball. So they used a small rock. They marked the goal with shoes. It didn't matter what they had. They just wanted to play.

Brazilians often have two last names. Neymar's first, da Silva, is his mother's last name. The second, Santos, is his father's last name. To make it simple, many Brazilians like Neymar are known by one name or a nickname.

Neymar Sr. hardly ever saw his son play. He was always working. But he heard about his son's amazing ability. He heard how his son was always playing against other boys much older and bigger.

Neymar Jr.'s life changed when he was about seven years old. Someone from the local futsal team came to his house. He wanted the young Neymar to play futsal. Futsal is a form of soccer. It is played on a hard court like one used for basketball.

Futsal helped Neymar develop his soccer skills. By the time he was 11, his fame had spread. Scouts from teams throughout Brazil came to watch him. One of them was from Santos Football Club (FC). It was Neymar Jr.'s favorite team. Brazilian soccer hero Pelé played most of his career there.

Futsal has six players per team, including the goalkeeper. It started in Uruguay in the 1930s. A coach was tired of practicing on rainy fields. So he found a way to play indoors. Futsal gets its name from two Spanish words. *Futbol* means "soccer." *Salon* means either "living room" or "indoor."

Neymar, *right*, tries to win the ball while playing with Santos in 2009.

Santos signed Neymar to play on its youth teams. By the time Neymar was 14, Real Madrid had invited him to play for its youth team in Spain. Real Madrid is one of the most famous soccer clubs in the world.

Neymar and his family visited Spain. But he decided to stay in Brazil and play with Santos.

Neymar

CHAPTER 2

BECOMING A PRO

Neymar had come a long way since joining Santos as an 11-year-old. He had moved up quickly through the youth teams. And when he was 17, he was finally ready to play with the senior team. He signed a contract to play for Santos as a professional.

Neymar made his debut on March 7, 2009. He came off the bench against Oeste FC. He started his first game eight days later. He scored a goal in

Neymar plays with Santos in the 2010 São Paulo state championship.

Neymar, *center*, fires a shot on net in the 2011 Copa Libertadores.

that game. He had 14 goals that year. Neymar was widely praised by fans, coaches, and sportswriters. When Neymar turned 18, his father allowed him to buy a car. He had the money to buy an expensive car. But instead he chose an ordinary Mini Cooper. He was often seen driving it around the city.

The following season, Neymar scored 42 goals. He led Santos to the São Paulo state league championship. Santos also won the Copa do Brasil. Top teams from around the world noticed Neymar. English Premier League team Chelsea FC offered to pay Santos $34.5 million to buy his contract. But he stayed with Santos.

He was becoming very famous and rich. He signed contracts in 2011 to promote major companies around the world. He earned millions of dollars.

Brazil's national soccer league is called the Campeonato Brasileiro Serie A. It is commonly known as just the Brasileiro. Teams also play in a knockout tournament called the Copa do Brasil. Each state in Brazil also has a tournament. São Paulo's is called the Paulista. Neymar helped Santos win three Paulista titles.

Later that year Neymar led Santos to the South American club championship. It's called the Copa Libertadores. In English that means the "Liberators of America Cup." He scored six goals in 13 games. He was named the tournament's best player.

Neymar

Neymar and his former girlfriend had a son in 2011. His name is David Lucca, or Davi. Neymar was 19 at the time. Davi and his mother moved to Barcelona in 2015 to be closer to Neymar.

Winning the Copa Libertadores qualified Santos to play for the Club World Cup. Neymar scored a goal to help his team reach the final. Santos played against FC Barcelona of Spain. Santos lost 4–0. But Neymar sparked the interest of Barcelona management.

On his twentieth birthday, Neymar scored his 100th goal. He had been playing for only three years. He scored 20 goals in the 2012 São Paulo state championship. That made him the top scorer. He also shared the top-scoring honor in the Copa Libertadores with eight goals.

Neymar finished 2012 with a major award. He was chosen as South America's Player of the Year.

Neymar, *left*, and a Santos teammate celebrate their 2010 Paulista title.

Neymar

CHAPTER 3

OFF TO EUROPE

eymar played four and a half seasons with Santos. He won many championships and awards. Big European teams noticed. They each wanted him at their clubs. Neymar dreamed of playing in Europe. Barcelona and Real Madrid from Spain and Chelsea from England were his favorites.

Neymar transferred to Barcelona in 2013. He had just turned 21. Barcelona is a world-famous club. He was happy. But he was sad about leaving his family.

Neymar holds the trophy honoring him as 2012 South American Player of the Year.

He cried when the Brazilian national anthem played before his final game with Santos.

Barcelona paid Santos more than $118 million to buy Neymar's contract. Transfers are common in soccer. Transfers are like player trades between teams. Neymar's was one of the most expensive ever. Neymar signed a new five-year contract with Barcelona. It paid him $15 million a year.

Barcelona was known for its star players. Several played for Spain's national team. Lionel Messi played for Argentina. Messi was the most famous player in the world.

Thousands of people cheered Neymar when he joined Barcelona. He signed his contract and went to practice. He jogged onto the field wearing his Barcelona jersey for the first time. A crowd of 56,500 people waiting for him at Barcelona's home stadium roared.

Some people worried Neymar was too skinny. They thought he wasn't big enough to play in the Spanish league. He was 5 feet 9 inches and weighed 142 pounds. The Barcelona

Neymar waves to the crowd at his introduction as a Barcelona player.

team doctor said he should add a few pounds. So Neymar hit the weights.

On the field, he quickly made an impact. He scored 14 goals in his first season. In his second season, he looked and played stronger. He had added 11 pounds. He scored 39 goals. And Barcelona won the Spanish league championship.

He also helped Barcelona win the European Champions League. It determines the best club team in Europe. Neymar scored a goal in the final. Barcelona defeated Italy's Juventus 3–1. It was Barcelona's first Champions League crown in four years.

Neymar is known for having a fierce temper. One of his worst moments came when he was 18. Santos coach Dorival Júnior stopped him from taking a penalty kick during a game. He wanted another player to take the kick. Neymar argued with Júnior and was suspended and fined.

Neymar was the eighth player to win the championships of both South America and Europe. He was the first player to score a goal in the final of both tournaments. His year wasn't done. He helped Barcelona win the 2015 Club World Cup in December.

Neymar finished third in the voting for World Player of the Year. The winner is chosen by players, coaches,

Neymar tries to beat a Real Madrid defender in a 2013 Spanish league match.

and sportswriters. In second place was Real Madrid's Cristiano Ronaldo. The winner was Neymar's teammate Messi.

Neymar continued to play well the next season. He scored another 31 goals in the 2015–16 season. Neymar helped Barcelona win another Spanish league championship.

Neymar

CHAPTER 4

SUCCESS WITH BRAZIL

Neymar is a hero in Brazil for his achievements with its national team. His international career began on Brazil's under-17 team. He scored a goal in the opening game of the 2009 Under-17 World Cup.

Many fans thought Neymar should have made Brazil's team for the 2010 World Cup. Former star players asked Coach Dunga to pick him for the team.

Neymar, *11*, celebrates his first goal with the Brazil senior team against the United States in 2010.

But Dunga felt Neymar was too young. Brazil lost in the World Cup quarterfinals. And Dunga was fired.

New Brazil coach Mano Menezes added Neymar to the team. He played his first game on August 10, 2010 against the United States in a friendly in New Jersey. He was only 18. His first senior goal was the game-winner as Brazil won 2–0.

Neymar next played for Brazil in the 2011 South American Youth Championship. He scored nine goals in nine games. Brazil won the title. Later that summer Neymar returned to the senior team. The Copa America was his first major tournament. It determines the champion of South America. He scored two goals, but Brazil again was beaten in the quarterfinals.

The player who wears the No. 10 jersey is often considered the best offensive player on the team. Pelé wore it when he led Brazil to three World Cup titles. Diego Maradona also wore it when he captained Argentina to the 1986 World Cup championship.

The 2012 Olympics were held in London. Brazil had never won a gold medal in soccer. Neymar scored three goals. One of

Neymar reacts after Brazil lost to Mexico in the 2012 Olympic final.

them came from a penalty kick in a 3–2 victory over Honduras in the quarterfinals. Brazil reached the final but lost to Mexico.

Neymar scored his first hat trick with Brazil only a month later. It was in a friendly. He had three goals in an 8–0 victory over China. By the summer of 2013, Neymar was given the honor of wearing the No. 10 jersey. He had been wearing No. 11.

The No. 10 jersey had been worn by Brazilian legends such as Pelé, Zico, and Ronaldinho. They all won World Cups.

Neymar salutes the home crowd after scoring a goal in the 2014
World Cup.

Neymar lived up to the high expectations that came
with the number. That same summer, Brazil played in the
Confederations Cup. It is a tournament for the champions of
each continent. Neymar scored four goals as Brazil won the
title. He was given the Golden Ball award as the tournament's
best player.

Neymar continued to improve. Many thought the 2014
World Cup in Brazil would be his big moment. He scored in two

of the first three games. He had the winning penalty kick to beat Chile in the second round.

But in the quarterfinals he was injured. Colombian defender Juan Zúñiga kneed him in the back. Neymar had to be carried off on a stretcher. He had broken a bone in his back. He was unable to play the rest of the World Cup. Brazil lost its next game to Germany 7–1.

Many people close to Neymar describe him as humble. He is devoted to his father and his son. He also is very religious. He put on a headband after winning the Olympic gold medal that said, "100% Jesus."

It took several weeks for Neymar to heal. He was made team captain when he returned. He was only 22. He celebrated by scoring four goals in a 4–0 victory over Japan. It was the first time he had scored four goals in a game for Brazil.

His next big test was the 2015 Copa America. It didn't go well. He scored a goal to give Brazil a 2–1 win over Peru in their

Neymar takes a penalty shot in a 2017 match against Real Sociedad.

first game. But after a 1–0 loss to Colombia in the second game, a fight broke out.

Neymar's temper got the best of him. He kicked the ball at Colombia's Pablo Armero. Another Colombian player accused him of a head butt. He was suspended from the Copa for four games. He was fined $10,000. It was his lowest moment on the national team.

But payback came in the summer of 2016. Neymar earned his way back onto the team in time for the Olympics. The Games took place on home soil in Rio de Janeiro. Neymar scored a goal as Brazil beat Colombia 2–0. Then he had two goals in a 6–0 win over Honduras in the semifinals.

After the 2016 Olympics, Neymar came back and had another stellar season at Barcelona. He had two goals in a 2017 Champions League match against Paris Saint-Germain FC. Neymar helped Barcelona erase a four-goal deficit and advance to the quarterfinals.

Next Brazil played Germany in the final. The entire country wanted revenge for the 7–1 loss at the 2014 World Cup. Neymar gave Brazil the lead in the first half. But Max Meyer tied it for Germany in the second. The game came down to penalty kicks. Neymar scored the last one to win the game for Brazil.

Neymar was already the most popular player in Brazil. He became a national hero when he won the gold medal. Brazil fans hope that he can top that by winning a World Cup title.

FUN FACTS AND QUOTES

- "They were very dismissive, the other boys. 'Who is this little kid?' … But I managed to convince them to let me play that first time, and I scored a goal. That changed their attitude." —Neymar on playing with older boys when he was younger

- Neymar was in a serious car crash when he was four months old. His father was driving with his mother on a steep mountain road in the rain. A car coming the other way hit them. Rescuers found Neymar under the seat of the car. He was cut by shattered glass and covered in blood.

- During his second season at Santos, Neymar and his friend Andres gave themselves new haircuts. The spiked look wasn't a hit with everyone. When his father saw him at a game, he was very upset. But Neymar scored two goals, and the hairstyle became immediately popular.

- "Now some are saying that Messi is better than Pelé. Well, he has to be better than Neymar first, which he isn't yet. He has more experience." —Brazilian soccer great Pelé on who is the greatest player of all time

WEBSITES

To learn more about Playmakers, visit **abdobooklinks.com**. These links are routinely monitored and updated to provide the most current information available.

GLOSSARY

contract
An agreement to play for a certain team.

cup
A trophy or a tournament. It is called a cup because many of the first trophies awarded to tournament winners were bowls or cups mounted on a small statue.

debut
First appearance.

final
The championship game of a tournament.

friendly
An exhibition game.

hat trick
When a player scores three goals in a game.

jersey
A soccer shirt.

knockout
A tournament format in which the losing team is eliminated.

league
A group of teams who regularly play each other.

penalty arc
A marked half-circle on top of the penalty area on a soccer field.

penalty kick
A play where a shooter faces a goalkeeper alone; it is used to decide tie games or as a result of a foul.

penalty spot
A small circle 12 yards (11 m) from the goal where the ball is placed for a penalty kick.

scout
A person whose job is to look for talented young players.

transfers
When players change teams.

INDEX

FURTHER RESOURCES

Jökulsson, Illugi. *FC Barcelona, More Than a Club.* New York: Abbeville Press Publishers, 2014.

Kortemeier, Todd. *Total Soccer.* Minneapolis, MN: Abdo Publishing, 2017.

Monnig, Alex. *Sports' Greatest Championships: The World Cup.* Minneapolis, MN: Abdo Publishing, 2013.